More tales of my Grandmother's
DREAMTIME

By NAIURA

BARTEL

DREAMTIME SYMBOLS
THEIR MEANINGS

ABORIGINAL ART may be of a spiritual nature, or a record of a tribal event, or a personal experience. It is expressed in painting, carving or chiselling, on whatever media is available. It can be as simple as hands stencilled on a rock face, a sign that records someone was once there—that they existed. If Aboriginal art was traditionally portrayed in the abstract, usually by untrained hands, today's graduates of Aboriginal art schools produce a variety of work using modern media techniques, yet retaining a sense of Aboriginality. Even so, traditional Aboriginal art remains readily available for purists. Some works have brief story-lines, others are left to the imagination. Here is a readers' guide to symbols used to illustrate the Dreaming. Though helpful for this book, it should not be considered comprehensive nor absolute because various tribal interpretations, or an individual's expression, are not rigidly bound.

Camp site or water hole		Windbreak	
Boomerang or clouds		Bushfire	
Man sitting		Digging stick	
Woman sitting		Shield	
River, creek etc		Hands (action)	
Spear		Eggs	
Dish		Animal tracks:	
Spear thrower		Kangaroo	
Track, path		Emu	
Man's footprints		Dingo	
Woman's footprints		Goanna	
Smoke or lightning		Snake	
Ants		Rain	

Published by Bartel Publications,
36 Rickety Street, Mascot, NSW, 2020, Australia
First published 2005

© copyright text and paintings by Naiura, 2005
Designed by Phillip Mathews Book Publishers
Printed by Everbest in China

ISBN 1-87-552022-8

Stephanie Miner

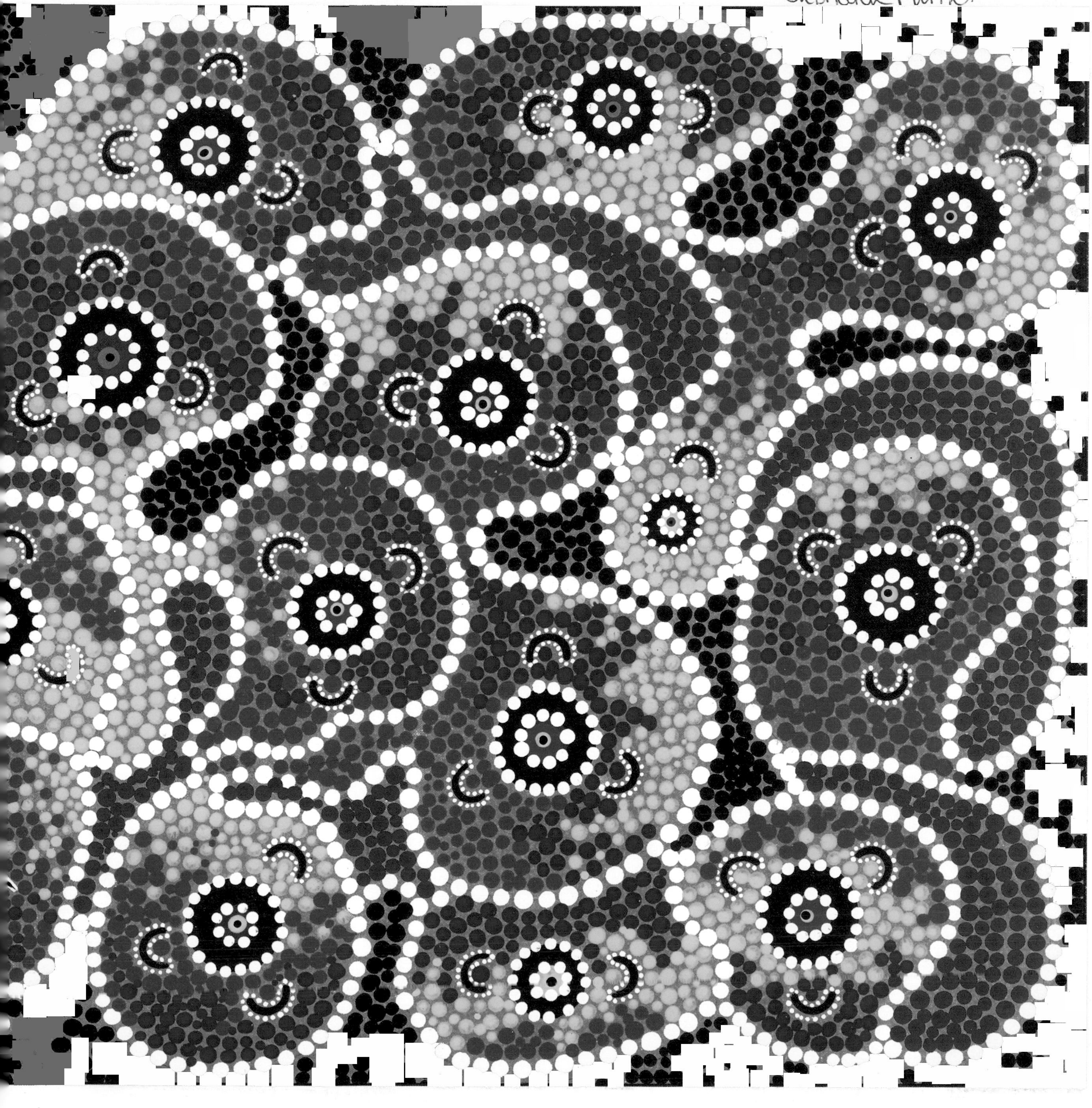

CONTENTS

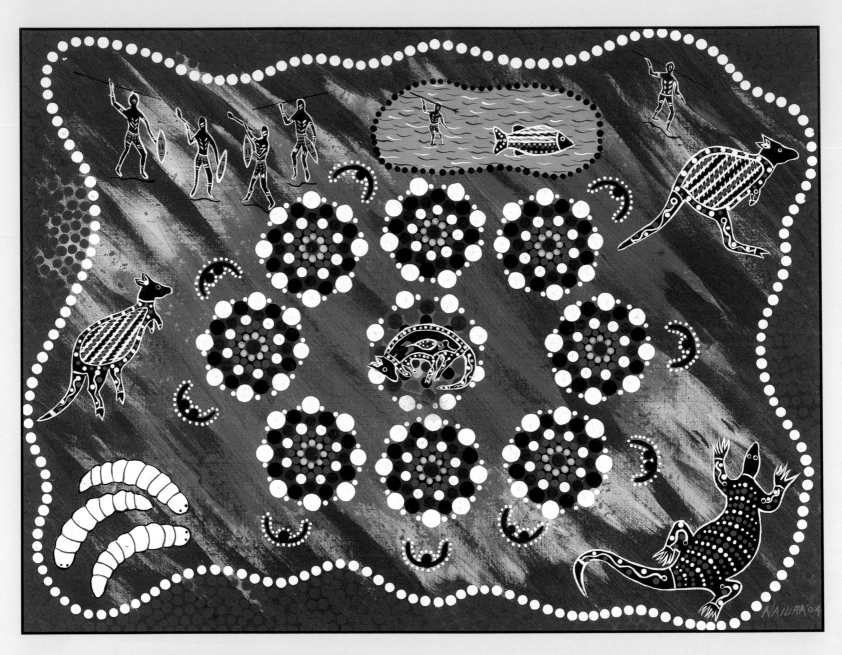

REFLECTIONS BY NAIURA ON THE DREAMING AS EXPLAINED TO HIM BY HIS GRANDMOTHER

THE DREAMING

AS TOLD BY NAIURA'S GRANDMOTHER

"THE Dreaming," said my grandmother long ago, "is our people's deep well of memory. It stores a wonderful mixture of sacred, mythical and practical ideas, passed on to us from our ancestors. Indeed, the Dreaming is the place where all our past exists, the place in which our thoughts, beliefs, and our sacred memories remain protected. Its wisdom explains to us the land, the sky, the sun and stars, just as it explains all living creatures: why they are what they are, how we relate to them, and how we should all share the landscape. For our people, the Dreaming is where all life began and it is the afterlife to which we go when our own time comes.

"Our mothers, fathers, grandmothers and uncles preserved the Dreaming for us, by re-telling the stories that their forebears once told them. We locked these stories in our memory so that we too may tell them to *our* children; and our children will one day tell their children who, in turn, will tell *their* children. That is how the Dreaming has existed beyond the memory of any single human being, for thousand upon thousands of years.

"Most stories of the Dreaming are shared by all who may listen, though some tribes have particular stories, events or myths that are theirs alone. At the heart of all these stories, however, are the shared beliefs that our people value.

"The form may be a simple guide to teach us, for instance, which plants, animals or places might be dangerous; or they may celebrate spirits, animals or places that deserve our respect. Some messages are complicated, such as how we should behave. Stories that remind us of tribal boundaries, rituals or taboos are very serious. Certain places, for instance, are too sacred to enter, and some mysteries are so secret that only grown men—or sometimes only women—may even discuss them.

"If stories retold explain the Dreaming to us, paintings add an individual's message. The most ancient records that speak directly to us are rock paintings. These may be a hand stencil to show someone was once there; or an animal once hunted; or, perhaps, a boundary dispute. Today, our people paint on bark, timber or canvas. Some are decorations in the traditional manner, but the best of them—for our people—are inspired by the Dreaming."

BAIAME'S REWARD
FOR THE HOSPITABLE BINJALI

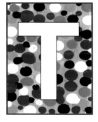THE territory of the Binjali people, a small inland tribe, was large but dry. Yet game was plentiful because the few small water holes there were big enough for their needs. But no lake or billabong big enough for fish had ever existed there. In fact, the Binjali had no name for fish because fish were unknown to them.

The Binjali people were as generous as they were well fed. When neighbouring tribes faced hardship or hunger, they always invited them to hunt on their land.

In time, however, neighbours began to abuse the Binjali's hospitality. They hunted on Binjali land so often—with or without permission—that the once plentiful game became so scarce that the Binjali themselves faced hunger. Forced for the first time to look beyond their land for food, the Binjali elders sought permission to hunt in their neighbours' territory. Yet despite the Binjali people's past generosity the neighbouring tribes refused them.

Their neighbours' ungrateful attitude so saddened the hungry Binjalis that they sat down and wept. Indeed, they cried for so long—and so loudly—that their mis-ery reached the ears of Baiame, the Great Spirit, and it troubled him. Their sadness so disturbed Baiame that he decided to reward the Binjali for having been a generous and law-abiding people.

Baiame did not stop them crying, however, quite the contrary: he encouraged their tears to flow across the large dust bowl in which they had all gathered. When the Binjali could cry no more, a vast lake of tears stretched around them.

The Great Spirit then filled that lake with big and tasty fish, all big enough for them to eat so that the Binjalis need never be hungry. The Binjali elders were overcome.

"We thank the Great Spirit for his gift," they said with shy respect, "though when our neighbours discover this lake they will eat all the fish till there are none left for our people, just as it has been in the past."

"Forget your fears," Baiame told the elders. "These fish are for the Binjali people alone. They will appear only to you. When others come to this lake they will find nothing, nothing but the bitter tears shed by the Binjali people they have so wronged!"

BAIAME'S REWARD FOR THE HOSPITABLE BINJALI

13

THE DOLPHIN KOOLYANGARA

AND A PRICE FOR DISOBEDIENCE

WHEN rains did not come the water holes were baked dry by a heat so searing that even the koolyangara, the children, grew listless. If the tribe was to survive, the elders decided, then it must move to the coast.

Despite the urgency, the tribe set out on the two-week journey at a measured pace, so that the elderly and the infants could keep up in the heat. The older koolyangara were far too excited by the prospect of seeing the sea for the first time to behave. They had to be constantly reminded to stay close.

The journey ended when the tribe camped at a fresh water spring near the sea. At last they could satisfy their burning thirst. When they sat to rest, however, three koolyangara were found to be missing. For children to explore without permission was cause enough for a scolding but this was much more serious. The tribe was in strange territory that even the elders had rarely visited.

When the children failed to respond to calls, the alarmed elders sent the tribe's best hunters to bring them in. They quickly found their tracks, which led to a ledge at the water's edge. There they ended, so the hunters searched along the shores, hoping to find them playing in the shallows but the shoreline cliffs rose sheer from deep water. There were no shallows. And no children.

When the hunters told the people that the children had disappeared, they cried and began their mourning song.

What the tribe would never know was that when the children arrived at the rock ledge, they had gazed in wonder at the sea they had never before seen. To them it seemed like an endless billabong, so they did what they always did in the billabongs of their homelands when it was too hot. They jumped in to play.

Too late they realised how deep it was. Too late they felt the power of the current that swept them away. Their cries were unheard by the tribe because they had strayed so far.

Only Boomali, a sea spirit, had heard them.

Boomali decided to save their lives but at a terrible price. He turned the disobedient koolyangara into dolphins. Certainly they could play in the sea now for as long as they wished—but they could never again leave it. The naughty koolyangara never saw their people again.

THE DOLPHIN KOOLYANGARA A PRICE FOR DISOBERDIENCE

DOOMAI
THE THIEF & THE NURUNDERI

OOMAI was unseen by the hunter, who placed his spears on the ground before wandering off to gather firewood. What wonderful spears, thought the envious Doomai, and how foolish to be so careless. Anyone could take them! Doomai could not take his eyes off the splendid spears till the hunter was well out of sight.

"He doesn't deserve such spears," muttered Doomai. "I would take much better care of them if they were mine..." Then, unable to control himself any longer, he gathered up the spears and ran back to the baanya, or camp.

Doomai, who thought he had slipped unnoticed into the baanya, was startled when a strange old man, who had arrived only the day before, approached him.

"Fine spears," said the old man.

"Very fine," boasted Dumai.

"And you made them?" asked the old man.

"Oh no," said Doomai. "They are a gift from a fool."

"A gift from a fool, eh?" said the old man, seemingly puzzled. "So, what did you give the fool in return?"

"I gave the fool nothing, of course" replied Doomai.

"In that case you stole them," said the old man, looking directly into Doomai's eyes.

"The fool left them unattended, so he didn't deserve them" protested Doomai, though he lowered his eyes.

"Is it so foolish to be trusting?" asked the old man.

"Well," said Doomai stubbornly, "they're mine now!"

"Oh no," said the old man, "they will never be yours. No matter how long you keep them they will always belong to the rightful owner. What they *will* be is a constant reminder that you are a thief."

The old man then turned his back and walked away.

Doomai felt such burning guilt that he returned to the hunter's camp that night. The sleeping hunter did not stir as Doomai crept close. Then the camp fire flickered, revealing the hunter's eyes. They were wide open, following Doomai's every move. Only when Doomai had replaced his spears did he stir, and only for a single nod.

Doomai fled. Glancing back to see if he was pursued he saw not the hunter watching from the camp fire but the strange old man. That stranger, he now realised, was Nurrunderi, the teacher, sent by Baiame, the Great Spirit.

DOOMAI THE THIEF & THE NURUNDERAI

THE KONINDERIE BILLABONG
THE RAINBOW WATERHOLE

 HE freshwater pool was hidden deep in the girraween, the place of flowers. It was called the Koninderie Billabong, or the Rainbow Water hole, because of the colours the many flowers reflected in its waters. Only certain fish, platypus, frogs, snakes, butterflies and beetles dwelt there, hidden away from all other creatures since time began.

All this changed one day when Yuaia, the frog, hopped in great alarm from the forest.

"Monsters!" he croaked. "Monsters are coming!"

The billabong creatures were amused by Yuaia's antics because no-one had *ever* found the secret billabong. But they choked on their laughter when Moodai and Bilana—a young man and young woman—ran from the bush. As the Koninderie creatures scattered to hide, these strange "monsters" sank to their knees and drank greedily from the sweet water.

Only Platypus was bold enough to risk a closer look at the monsters. He swam deeply but surfaced too soon and found himself face to face with Moodai! Frightened, Platypus turned to dive, but the monster called him.

"Are you *another* spirit?" called Moodai, who had never seen a platypus.

"A spirit! Me? " said Platypus. "Of course not."

"But the frog," said Moodai, "surely he's a spirit?"

"Yuaia? He's a corroboree frog!" said Platypus, confused. In the pause that followed, both were too afraid to move.

"What sort of monsters are you?" said Platypus, finally.

"We're not monsters, we're lovers!" said Moodai. "Lovers no-one wants. We're from different tribes, you see, and tribal law forbids us to wed. Both our tribes drove us off and we've been lost for weeks. We had nearly perished from thirst when we spotted the strange frog, which we supposed must be a spirit. Following him, spirit or not, saved us. At least for the moment."

"Will you drive us off?" he added. "We'll perish if you do."

Platypus listened carefully, then slipped away to speak with the other creatures of the Rainbow Waterhole. When he returned, he spoke solemnly to Moodai and Bilana:

"You may stay only if you *never* reveal our secret place."

Moodai and Bilana agreed and remained forever. And where is this secret place? That answer lies in the question.

THE KONINDERIE BILLABONG THE RAINBOW WATERHOLE

BARALGA & DINEWAN

 THE BROGLA AND EMU

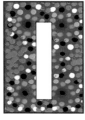I N the beginning, Baiame, the Great Spirit, created both male and female creatures, but he left it to them to find each other to marry.

Nobody knows why Baralga, the brolga, was so unaware of how it all worked. Perhaps he was too busy admiring his reflection in the lakes—his fine feathers, long bill and slender legs upon which he danced so lightly.

Baralga longed, nevertheless, for someone to share his dance and soared the skies in his search. One day, he spotted Dinewan, the emu, running swiftly across the plain.

"You could put your powerful legs to better use by dancing with me," he called from above.

Dinewan stopped dead, hardly believing his ears. His big eyes blinked wide in amazement when Baralga landed beside him and began to dance.

"What *are* you doing!" he demanded angrily.

"I'm dancing," said Baralga, "and you may join me."

"Dance?" scoffed Dinewan. "Emus don't dance. We run!"

"Then I shall teach you," said Baralga.

"For what possible reason?" snorted Dinewan.

"So we might marry and then dance together forever."

"You *are* mad," said Dinewan. "Emus not only never dance, they never marry brolgas. And I'm a male, anyway!"

"Does that make a difference?" asked Baralga, puzzled.

"Males *never* marry males," replied Dinewan angrily.

"Needn't stop us dancing, though," said Baralga.

The stubborn birds argued, beak to beak, all day.

"Why do you argue so," a voice scolded gently.

Neither bird turned but Dinewan stamped his foot.

"This fool wants to marry me despite my telling him that brolgas don't marry emus."

"Of course not," agreed the stranger, sounding amused. "Brolgas marry only brolgas."

When the two angry birds turned to the stranger, they faced the most beautiful brolga that Baralga had ever seen. (She was also the *only* other brolga he had ever seen.)

"And do you dance?" said Baralga, his voice strangely shy.

"Of course," said the brolga, "I am a very good dancer."

"Then perhaps *we* might marry," said Baralga, hopefully.

"Perhaps," said the brolga and, stretching her wings, she joined Baralga in a very beautiful, very dainty, dance.

Dinewan stretched his legs, too. He fled!

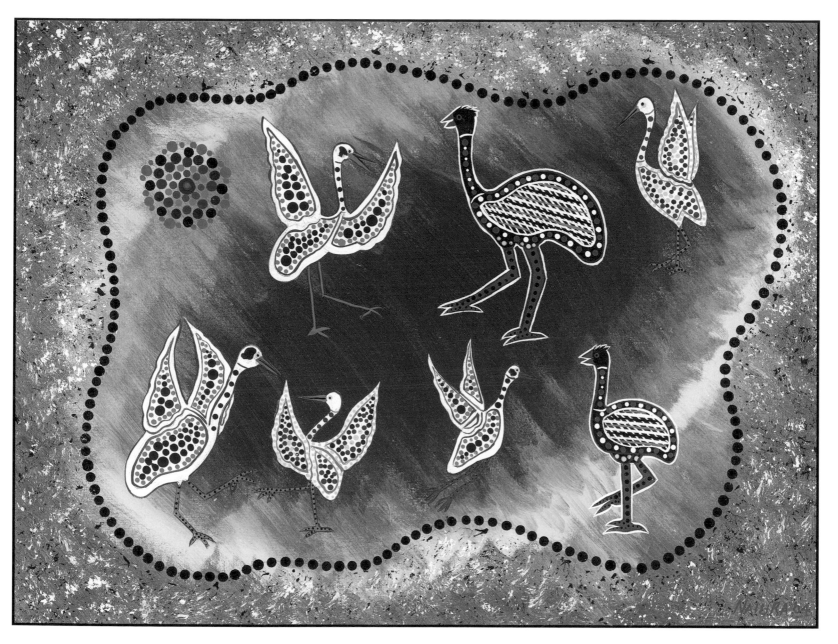

BARALGA & DINEWAN THE BROLGA AND THE EMU

THE TRESPASSERS

AND THEIR GRIM FATE

HE two young hunters seemed always to have a kangaroo or a wallaby on their shoulders when they returned to the *baanya*, or camp. They boasted loudly about their hunting but their people, ever grateful for the food, always welcomed them.

So successful became the young hunters, and for such a long period, that the elders took notice. They too were good hunters—and much more experienced—yet none could recall such good fortune, especially when the game in their territory was so sparse. When curiosity grew to suspicion, the elders sent a man to track them.

The next day the young hunters returned yet again with meat, boasting that the tribe might starve without them.

They did not notice the old tracker slip back into camp and whisper to the elders. What he whispered confirmed the elders' worst fears: the hunters had been crossing into their neighbour's tribal land to pursue *their* game. Trespassing on another's land was such a serious breach of tribal law that if the offended tribe ever learnt of it there would be very serious trouble for them all. Their good fortune, the elders realised, was not the plentiful meat that the young hunters had brought them but that their neighbours had not yet spotted them!

When the elders approached the hunters, they congratulated them but with a sly caution.

"Always be careful where a hunt may lead you because it is forbidden to cross the boundaries of a neighbour's land without their permission—and ours," they said.

"Oh, we would never do that," said the hunters, "we observe tribal law in every way."

This lie saddened the elders because the punishment for trespassing was banishment from the tribe. In fact they were too sad to banish them because the foolish young men were still their kin, though they had wronged the tribe.

Baiame, the Great Spirit, who had watched the breach of tribal law, expected the elders to deal with it. When he saw that their grief made the task too hard for them, he waited to see if the young hunters dared cross the boundaries again. When they did, Baiame acted firmly. He turned one into a kangaroo and the other into a wallaby, a punishment worse even than banishment—because now the offended tribe would hunt *them*!

THE TRESPASSERS AND THEIR GRIM FATE

THE ELUSIVE BINDAR
THE MYSTERIOUS KANGAROO

E VEN the oldest member of the tribe could remember the mysterious bindar. All had tried to catch it when they were younger men, just as their grandfathers had—and with no better luck. It was no surprise to them when the eager young hunters returned to the baanya and spoke with confusion of the mysterious bindar. Their uncles laughed loudly when the boys explained how they had trapped the bindar in a cave from which there could be no escape, yet somehow it had. Or how they had tracked it for hours only to find its tracks ended suddenly at a sheer rock face.

Wirrinun, the wise man, called to the young men.

"What nonsense you talk," he scoffed. "Only a bird's tracks could end at a sheer rock face. What sort of hunters pretend that a bindar can escape from the inescapable?"

"But it's true," wailed the young men, stung by the Wise Man's words, though unwilling to show disrespect. As for their uncles' amusement, it made them even more determined to catch the bindar.

So, the young hunters tried ever harder. Yet though their hunting improved to the point that they managed to catch fresh meat almost daily, the bindar still eluded them—to the growing amusement of their uncles.

When the Wirrinun beckoned one night for the young hunters to approach the elders' fire, they expected more teasing. They were surprised when asked to be seated.

"So, again you failed to catch the bindar..." began Wirrinun, rasing his hands to silence their protests about the bindar's great cunning. The Wise Man then turned to the elders around the fire.

"Elders," he said, "did any of you ever catch the mysterious bindar?" One by one the elders shook their heads.

"Nor did I," added Wirrinun. Then, turning back to the young hunters, he spoke to them affectionately, as children.

"You see, *koolyangara*, that maddening bindar is none other than Nurrunderi, the spirit teacher. He appears to us to tease us *only* when we first begin to hunt. It is his way, because pursuing him teaches us to be much better hunters so that our families need never experience the pain of hunger."

Glancing at three wallabies that the young men had placed by the fire, Wirrinun turned again to the elders.

"Nurrunderi has taught them well," he said with satisfaction.

THE ELUSIVE BINDAR THE MYSTERIOUS KANGAROO

JAYAWAH'S LESSON
KURRIA IN THE BILLABONG

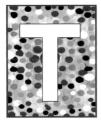 THE people had travelled for many days to reach the billabong, as they did every year. It was a good place for the tribe to camp during the colder months. So many animals watered there that game was always plentiful. Or it was before Kurria, the giant crocodile, took up residence.

The elders, anxious to protect their people, sent the tribe's boldest warriors to kill the crocodile. But Kurria was much too strong for them, and too wily. So the elders decided that their only hope was to drive all other animals from the water hole till Kurria became so hungry that he would have to leave it to find food. Meantime, the elders warned, their people must keep well clear of the billabong.

There were, nevertheless, those who could not resist their curiosity for a glimpse of the monster. This led children to copy them until threats from their parents stopped it. All, that is, except for the twins, a boy and girl who crept so often to the billabong that the patient Kurria, waiting just below the surface, expected to eat them. The twins, however, were not only naughty but cunning. They constantly tormented Kurria by approaching the water then running back, never pausing quite long enough to be caught.

In time, the elders' plan took its toll. Kurria became so hungry in the now deserted billabong that he crept away one night to search for a more tempting water hole.

The twins, who did not know Kurria had gone, returned to torment the monster. There was something else they did not know: Jayawah, a water spirit, had decided that the twins deserved a lesson for disobeying the elders and tormenting an animal. Taking the form of Kurria, he rose to the surface as the twins approached to tease him. The twins, as always, timed their flight to the last moment, but this time found themselves unable to run. Jayawah's had cast his spell. He then leapt from the water and swallowed the twins whole.

Jayawah kept the twins in his belly for so long that, when he released them, their people had grown old that their parents, uncles and aunties had long since died. Those of the tribe that remained were now strangers, who drove the twins away to live all alone.

The twins spent the rest of their lives teaching children who visited of the need to obey the elders and to respect all animals, until they too went to the Dreaming.

JAYAWAH'S LESSON KURRIA IN THE BILLABONG

YALUNGA
THE RAINBOW SERPENT

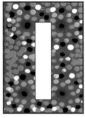N a dark cave, far beneath the ground, lies a very deep, red lake where Yalunga lives, the Rainbow Serpent.

Yalunga's *baanya*, or camp, is unlike any other. It is not even on solid ground but deep within the lake itself. The Rainbow Serpent, you see, cannot exist without water, which is why Yalunga appears above ground only when it rains, or when the air is very moist. When he does, the Rainbow Serpent casts a beautifully coloured arc in the sky, or across a misty gully, though often only briefly.

No one really knows how Yalunga leaves his baanya to paint his beautiful colours in the sky, or even why. Some tribes believe he does it to watch over their people. Those who behave well, please him well; those who do not, he swallows! And those he swallows, so they say, are taken back to his baanya to live out their lives in its gloom and darkness.

Others say that Yalunga sometimes chooses to rest in the landscape rather than return to his baanya. He may sleep in a damp cave or under a wet rock ledge. Almost any wet, dark place might do, so long as the sun cannot find him. If the sun ever did, so it is said, it would fade the Rainbow Serpent away, perhaps forever. Anyone foolish enough to disturb Yalunga's hiding place risked making him angry enough to swallow them.

Some tribes go further, claiming that all people who drown have been swallowed by the Rainbow Serpent. Not everyone believes this, though they realise it makes a good story with which to warn children of the dangers that lurk in deep water holes or in tidal currents.

Some tribes go much further even than that! They believe that Yalunga, the Rainbow Serpent, is so powerful that he created all things.

The Rainbow Serpent's powers are different for different tribes. Some even pronounce his name differently. All know who he is, however, and all are in awe of him.

YALUNGA THE RAINBOW SERPENT

THE GOOGARH
& THE ORPHANS

THE baby googarhs, or goannas, were quite alone after the hunter had taken their mother. Yet though their prospects were grim, because they had not yet learned to fend for themselves, the most pressing thoughts on their childish minds were about play.

In time, nevertheless, they grew very hungry. They had found and tasted some insects and grubs without any satisfaction before a strangely familiar smell filled their nostrils. The delicious scent led them to a carcass—a favoured googarh food!—but they were halted in their tracks by the fierce hissing of a female goanna that was already feeding there.

Had the baby goannas been older they would have learned never to approach another goanna while it was feeding. Not only would it fiercely protect its meal but it might well choose to eat *them* as well. The little googarhs, however, who knew nothing of this, and kept approach-ing the angry adult with soft hissing sounds asking, in effect, to be fed. After a while, this triggered a remark-able response from the adult, who allowed them to ap-proach. When the nervous babies stopped just short of her, hissing very softly now, she recognised their fear and backed away a little, responding with similarly soft hiss-ing sounds. Only then did the baby googarhs dare feed, and they ate ravenously.

The googarhs never knew quite how lucky they were.

Only two days earlier the female goanna had laid her eggs in an abandoned brush turkey's nest but a *nuraword-dubununa,* a carpet snake, had discovered and devoured them. The unhappy female had been searching for a mate to help her lay more eggs when she had found the car-cass. Thus, when the baby googarhs had approached, the strong motherly feelings she felt for her own lost eggs overcame all hostility. Not only did she decide not to eat the baby googarhs, she chose instead to adopt them.

THE GOOGARH AND THE ORPHANS

KRANGALANG

THE CONFIDENT CRAB

KRANGALANG, the crab, was such a confident juvenile that he never felt any need for the help or advice of his elders. So sure of himself was he that he never felt any need to think beyond the moment. When he was hungry, he knew where to find food; and he always did. The thought that it might run out some day never entered his head. He was just as confident about safety, too, always the last to hide when danger threatened. And why not? He could always find a hole in which to conceal himself or a rock beneath which he could shelter until danger passed. Though repeatedly warned by his elders that he might leave it too late one day, Krangalang scoffed at the suggestion.

One day, when Krangalang had wandered well beyond his normal territory, he became so excited by the new surroundings that he failed to notice a very big fish moving slowly and menacingly towards him. It was already close when Krangalang spotted it, though his confidence remained as high as ever as he dug sharply at the ground in order to bury himself.

But he could not bury himself. It was not sand beneath him, like his normal territory, but solid rock! With no hope of digging, he looked wildly around for a crack or overhang that might hide him. There were none.

Wild panic gripped Krangalang as he scuttled back and forth across the rock in a futile search for a place to hide. There was nowhere to be found and the big fish kept coming! Finally, Krangalang flattened himself against the rock bed to await his fate in helpless terror.

The fish cast a great dark shadow as it hovered above Krangalang, opening and closing a gaping jaw as it inspected him. Then, ever so slowly, it moved on.

Krangalang did not move for a very long time. He had been spared, he realised, by the only possibility in the sea's food chain that could have saved him. Crabs were not part of that big fish's diet.

It was a very different Krangalang who returned to his normal habitat. He was noticeably more attentive of his elders. Indeed, he was markedly more careful about everything, particularly his safety.

KRANGALANG THE CONFIDENT CRAB

THE KONINDERIE WEEDAH

THE RAINBOW BOWER BIRD

NY tribe fortunate enough to live in such fertile land should surely have been contented. There was ample fresh water and the hunting was easy. Reeds, with which to make baskets, were plentiful, as were small trees from which strong, straight spears could be fashioned.

Yet for reasons no-one remembered, the tribes' people chose to isolate themselves in separate camps. Far from being happy, they seldom spoke to each other. When they did, it usually led to angry arguments or silly bickering.

The spirits, well aware of this foolishness, had let the tribe be, hoping that the people would in time come to their senses and behave better towards each other. At first, Baiame, the Great Spirit, having provided all that most tribes would need for an agreeable life of comfort, was disappointed. In time, however, their ingratitude made him so impatient that he was obliged to act.

Only when a *weedah*, or bower bird, arrived in their midst—speaking their own language—did the foolish people stop shouting insults at each other. To their astonishment, the weedah circled the camps scattered across the tribe's land, summoning the people to a meeting with a voice so powerful that all felt bound to obey.

The assembled tribe watched as the weedah then began to slowly circle their land. Their wonder turned to growing alarm, however, when its feathers began to absorb the rich colours of the landscape while the land, which had been so lush and colourful, grew correspondingly dull. By the time the weedah had completed its circle it was transformed into a splendidly coloured *koninderie weedah*, a rainbow bowerbird, but the beautiful land, which had surrendered its colour, had become a drab desert.

Realising that the weedah was a spirit, the people wailed:

"Oh, we shall surely starve now! All the plants have withered and the animals we depend on will leave our land."

"A tribe that loses all desire for unity deserves to be punished," replied the koninderie weedah. "If you learn to work together instead of squabbling you will not starve. But you are doomed to roam far across this now barren land in search of food until you regain proper respect for one and other. That is what Baiame, the Great Spirit, taught your elders. Now you must learn for yourselves."

THE KONINDERIE WEEDAH THE RAINBOW BOWER BIRD

BURRAGINYA

THE SELFISH HUNTER

URRAGINYA's hunting skills were the envy of all. He was by far the best in the tribe, yet no-one admired him. The problem was that he would never share, no matter how successful his hunt. Fortunately this had little effect on his people's welfare because his brothers were fine hunters, though his selfishness saddened them. After all, any food brought back to camp belonged to everyone, even visiting strangers. That was the custom, the tradition of sharing being older than the memory of the oldest elder—and it was taught to the young at a very early age.

In time, Burraginya's great skills—and his selfishness—became known to other tribes, and eventually throughout the land. The spirits noticed, too, though none interfered, expecting Burraginya's attitude to surely soften. As time passed, however, the only change in Burraginya's ways was that he grew ever more selfish.

The patient spirits realised that his conduct could no longer be ignored. If Burraginya's ways were allowed to continue, other headstrong hunters might be tempted to follow his example. Such selfishness, were it to spread, would lead to terrible hardship for the all the people, because so many depended as much on the sharing as the skills of the hunters in their tribes. Burraginya would be offered one last chance to mend his ways.

One evening, as Burraginya was cooking, far from the tribe's camp, a spirit approached his fire from out of the darkness. It was in the form of a very old man.

"I have not eaten for days and I am hungry," said the spirit. "Would you share your meat with me?"

"Hunt your own," snapped Burraginya.

"But I have hunted for many days ," said the spirit, "I am old and my skills are slow... and I need very little."

Burraginya, was unmoved and again refused angrily.

It was Burraginya's last act of selfishness because the spirit sent him directly to Bullima, the land of the spirits. There he was condemned to hunt meat and gather roots for them all for the rest of his life. And the spirits had huge and demanding appetites.

Burraginya was so foolish that he never understood why such a clever hunter should so anger the spirits. That selfishness was his downfall never occurred to him.

BURRAGINYA THE SELFISH HUNTER

GULNYAN'S REWARD
FOR DISOBEDIENCE

FTER his bora, or initiation, Gulnyan's character would normally have been developed by learning tribal law, behaviour and bushcraft—especially hunting—from an elder. The elder was usually a father or an uncle, their longer experience of life and lore being regarded the best teacher.

Gulnyan, however, felt no need for advice. His first move was to separate himself from tribal hunting parties to hunt alone. To the surprise and delight of everyone, he proved himself a capable hunter. In the months that followed he returned often with meat for the tribe, even when the more experienced hunters had fared poorly.

Gulnyan misunderstood the praise he received. Instead of appreciating it as encouragement, which was the elder's intention, he saw it as an acknowledgement that he was now the best hunter. It was a vain attitude but the elders were patient, putting it down to Gulnyan's youth.

The other hunters, who continued to encourage him, asked how he managed to track so many animals in a single day, but Gulnyan refused to explain. This silence troubled them, not least because it ignored tribal lore, it

being customary for hunters to share all their knowledge of game for the common good.

A young man flouting of tribal lore so soon after initiation was bound to arouse the curiosity of the *wirrinun*, the wise man, who decided he should secretly follow Gulnyan. That hunt led them to a distant clearing, where many types of animals grazed in peace. When the wirrinun recognised the clearing, he was very angry. It was a sacred place, respected by all of the region's tribes, where animals lived in safety under the protection of Baiame, the Great Spirit. It was obvious now why Gulnyan had been so successful but why, wondered the wirrinun, had Baiame not punished him. He did not have to wonder long because a terrible voice thundered across the clearing.

"How many times must you be warned never to hunt these creatures," it roared. "I have been patient because of your youth but now you must pay the price."

Then, as the wirrinun watched, Gulnyan gradually turned into a bindar, or kangaroo.

"As you have hunted, so now shall you be hunted," said Baiame. "Now leave. You don't deserve my protection!"

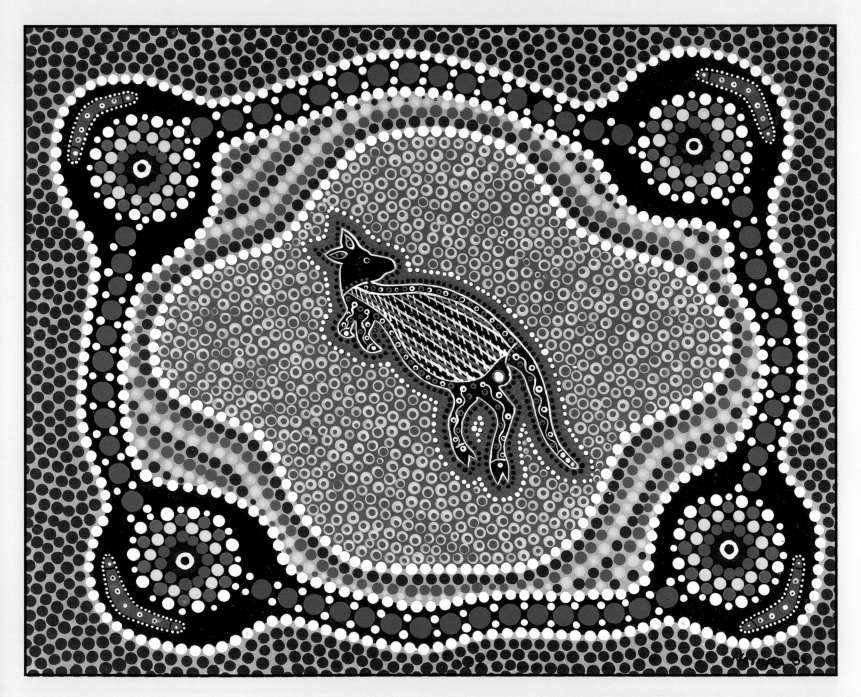

GULNYAN'S REWARD FOR DISOBEDIENCE

GOOROOGANDU
THE HOMELESS SPIRIT

IT began long ago when a weary, homeless spirit, called *Gooroogandu*, stumbled into the land of the Djurabal people. It was as disrespectful then as it is today to enter any tribe's land without permission, so the Djurabal people confronted him.

"My bad manners," apologised Gooroogandu, "were unintended, the result of weariness. I have travelled so long and so far in my search for a home."

Then, with suitable formality, he asked the Djurabal people if they would be so kind as to let him live there.

The Djurabal people refused. Without thought or kindness, they ordered him to leave at once.

There it might have ended, had Gooroogandu somewhere to go. But since he did not, he reacted stubbornly, and set about making a camp fire. This so enraged the Djurabal that they threatened to spear his legs. And when the spirit continued to ignore them, they began to beat him with their boomerangs.

Gooroogandu, deeply offended, invoked his spiritual powers to protect himself. Standing proudly erect, he absorbed all blows till the boomerangs became parts of his body. One boomerang, magically, became part of his back; another, his belly; and yet another, his feet. Their beating had not so much hurt him as transformed him—blow-by-blow—into a very different creature. The spirit now resembled a fish!

"Yes," said Gooroogandu, as the beaters recoiled in alarm, "you have beaten me into a fish! Since I'm so unwelcome on your land, I shall live in your billabong."

"Go then, go!" They shouted very loudly, because the spirit frightened them.

As it should have, because their rejection so saddened Gooroogandu as he swam in the billabong that he could not stop weeping. Indeed, his tears became so bitter that they turned the sweet waters of the billibong to salt water.

Soon, all the fish died, which caused hunger. And when all the animals left the land in search of fresh water to drink, the Djurabal hunters were unable to find enough game to feed the tribe.

In time, hunger forced the Djurabal off their once hospitable land. They were never to be heard of again, remembered only for their unkindness to a homeless stranger.

GOOROOGANDU THE HOMELESS SPIRIT

BUROOGANDI

& THE SPIRIT WITHIN

BEING painfully shy, Buroogandi never drew attention to himself. He rarely spoke, and never in defiance, even when teased. Though it concerned his friends they did not interfere, because his shyness seemed not to worry him.

How different was the truth, though Buroogandi was much too meek to express it. His shyness troubled him to the point at which he doubted he had any courage at all.

When the time for his *bora* approached—the initiation into manhood—Buroogandi grew so tormented that he approached the wiseman. The *wirrinun* listened carefully, patiently too, because Buroogandi was so hesitant that it took much of the day to explain his self-doubt.

"It is your spirit, Buroogandi," said the wirrinun, finally.

"What spirit, Uncle?" said Buroogandi. "I have none!"

"Oh, everyone has a spirit," said the wirrinun. "It is our spirit that controls our thoughts, our feelings and our behaviour. We could not exist without our spirit ."

"So, what is my spirit like, Uncle?" said Buroogandi.

"That I cannot answer for you," he replied. "Your spirit is anything *you* imagine it to be. If you imagine it to be a timid dove, then a timid dove you shall be."

Buroogandi left, overcome with self-pity, for a timid dove he clearly was. Yet when alone and unseen, Buroogandi often felt bolder, if only a little. So, when he was sure no-one could hear, he shouted his misery at the sky.

There a flash caught his eye. It was bilyara, the eagle, circling high. And when the sun's struck its wing tips they seemed, at such a distance, to catch fire. Dazzled by this splendid sight, the wirrinun's words rang in Buroogandi's head. "Your spirit is anything you imagine it to be…"

Buroogandi sucked in breath and squared his shoulders.

"My spirit shall *not* be that of a timid dove," he cried to the sky, "I shall be bilyara, the powerful eagle, with wings of fire." But these, as yet, were only words.

When the bora ceremony began, the tribe was uneasy. Might Buroogandi, they wondered, be too shy even to dance? Tension rose when Buroogandi remained motionless as the others began their dance. At last, he moved. Yet he did not dance as the others did: not as a kangaroo nor an emu nor a brolga. When Buroogandi danced it was as the powerful bilyara, spreading wings of fire for all to admire. Buroogandi's spirit had risen to "what he imagined it to be". And it remained with him for life.

BUROOGANDI & THE SPIRIT WITHIN